MW00325940

K.RASHAD

THE

Journey

BACK

TO

Self

TAKE A DEEP DIVE WITHIN

Instagram @K__Rashad

The Journey Back To Self: Take A Deep Dive Within by K. Rashad

March 2023

www.PinkButterflyPressllc.com

Front cover artist: agsandrew

Back cover artist: agsandrew

Pink Butterfly Press LLC.

Introduction page.

When I started writing the Love Isn't Constant Pain series, my aim was to help others heal and love themselves. While writing the series, I did so much reflecting and healing myself. Before I started the series, I was in a dark place mentally and emotionally. My grandma was sick, slowly losing her life, and my mother had cancer at the time, fighting for her life. I was also losing the battle that was going on within me. I drifted off and lost myself along the way. In this book, I share with you my journey back to self. I share with you my weakest moments, my darkest days, my mistakes, and the lessons I've learned. When your back is against the wall, and life is too much to deal with, sometimes you must step away, separate yourself, and take "The Journey Back To Self." – K.Rashad

Opening Page.
7/25/2018

I remember the dark days before I started my journey back to myself. I thought I would never have made it out. At the time, I felt God was punishing me. It's crazy how your whole life could change and fall apart in the blink of an eye. We see people smiling daily and assume they are happy and living their best lives, but we don't see the battles they face behind closed doors. We have no idea that they are barely hanging on behind that smile. Sometimes, I look back at some of the old work I wrote during the darkest days of my life. I want to share one called "Suffering Internally".

I am not a broken man. But I need some help and clarification, exhausted. Mentally and emotionally drained. I was drowning in my sorrows and pain and haunted by all my mistakes. Battle after battle, fight after a fight: long days and restless nights. I barely sleep, haven't had much appetite, and hardly eat. Some days I feel everything. Some days I feel nothing at all. They come to me with questions as if I have all the answers. They seem to forget I'm just a man even though I don't know it all. "You're so well put together", they say. Little do they know I'm falling apart on the inside. Suffering internally, and facing my most challenging battles. Also, my inner demons have their way with me. How can one man take on so much?

Sometimes you have to block out the world's noise to hear yourself.

Intuition.

Here we are again. Not back where we started, but much further ahead. It's never over; there will always be parts of ourselves we need to heal. There will always be some lessons to learn. I told you the self-love journey never ends. We simply learn how to handle our situations better. The more we get to know ourselves, the better we are at handling our problems. Not only do we learn to accept ourselves, we also learn to accept people for who they are. We see people for who they are, and we no longer lose ourselves by trying to change them. We become better at deciding who belongs in our lives and who doesn't. It's easier to point out who's worth it and who isn't. We learn to trust ourselves more and listen to our intuition.

I looked in the mirror and saw everyone else's reflection in me, making it hard to truly see myself.

Mirroring.

I used to be too quick to judge people, but then I looked back at who I was and all my mistakes. The man I was before I started this journey and how I was set in my ways. I've learned to forgive myself for not knowing what I know now. You might need more time to get the answers to your question; some answers come further along your journey. As you walk it, everything starts to unfold and slowly make sense. Many people aren't broken; many are just lost and struggling to find their way. The journey is much more challenging when you feel like nobody understands you and you have nobody to turn to. I don't believe people hurt people intentionally. They mirror the people who have hurt them in their lives. Most people want to do better, become better people, and want to heal. However, some people need help knowing where to start or how to.

You'd be surprised how many adults suffer from co-dependency and abandonment issues, making being alone hard for them.

Time Alone.

As hard as it may be, it would be best if you went through a season of loneliness. First, we must learn to enjoy being comfortable in our own company. Spending time with ourselves is an essential part of the self-love journey. It allows us to reflect on past relationships and take an honest, in-depth look at ourselves. That season of loneliness allows us to heal properly. However, the beginning stage is always the hardest. It involves a lot of mental work. A poisoned mind is just as bad, if not worse, than a broken heart. It takes a lot of strength, but we must accept and be willing to allow things to fall apart; we must die to be born again. Take a deep dive within. Who you were, you can no longer be. Are you ready to release and separate yourself from everything and everyone? Yes, it's hard and painful, but the light you'll find at the end of the tunnel is beautiful; light won't be the only thing you'll find. You'll find an unconditional love that has always been within you. As hard as it may be, it would be best if you went through a season of loneliness; it comes with the journey. The journey back to yourself.

"

During that season
of loneliness,
I found comfort
in my own company.

My Own
Best Friend.

People could live their whole lives never meeting or knowing their true selves. We think we know it all, only to find out later that we know nothing. I spent years unlearning, learning, and getting to know myself. I've put in at least a decade of inner work, and I'm still doing it. The journey never ends, and healing is never done. Every other day, I was getting to know a new me; the weak me, the strong me, the happy me, the sad me, the misunderstood and lost me, the hurt and angry me. I spent time alone with every part of me. One by one, I got to know them; it was like interviewing myself. They all were a part of me. I wanted us all to be one big happy family, but how could I make that happen if I didn't understand why they all were the way they were? Slowly, I was becoming comfortable with being alone. Isolation didn't feel like isolation anymore because I was becoming my best friend.

The more you heal,
the smaller your circle
gets. You start realizing
you don't need anybody
but yourself.

Detachment And Separation.

Losing yourself is a part of growth, but losing people is the most challenging aspect of healing and building a healthier relationship with yourself. You lose friends, lovers, and family members as well. Detaching yourself from people who no longer serve you is hard. Not everyone will like or understand that where you're at right now, you need yourself the most. Many people aren't going to respect the new healthy boundaries you've set, and some people will even make you feel guilty for doing what's best for you. You'd be surprised by how some people react when they no longer have access to you instead of supporting you and seeing it as something you must do for yourself. They look at it as if you've changed or are just too good to be around them anymore when that's not even true. A lot of hatred and jealousy comes with doing what's best for you. Friendships and relationships will start falling apart; family members will begin distancing themselves from you. You'd think they would be proud of the new you, but not those who have never wanted what's best for you and can no longer manipulate, hinder your growth, or take from you.

Releasing all the wrong people in your life frees up space and allows all the right people to enter your life. You must be open to change, peace, love, and happiness. Sometimes you must step back and look at all the things and people blocking you from experiencing a new beginning.

At the time,
I didn't understand
what was going on.
My whole world was
falling apart, and
I was losing my
mind trying to keep
everything together.

Ego Death,
Surrender.

God stripped everything from me. I've spent years feeling trapped and isolated. Everything was at a standstill, and all doors were shut; nothing would move for me. It was time for me to surrender. As much as I hate to admit it, I was losing my mind trying to control things I no longer had control over. I realized that doing things my way wasn't always the best. I had to push my feelings and pride aside. Finally, he left me with no other choice but to look within.

I could no longer block out the voices, and no one was around me to distract me from facing the truth. I've spent most of my life lying to myself. It was time to be honest with myself.

Darkness And Truth.

It would help if you went through a season of darkness. But, unfortunately, spending time alone is only sometimes as peaceful as people make it seem. Being alone with your thoughts is when the real battle starts. While in isolation, you notice things about yourself and people you've never seen. When you get rid of all distractions, reality starts to set in. The truth reveals itself. Truth we've spent most of our lives ignoring, running, and hiding from. Truth we don't want to see or hear. We are not ready to accept the truth because we've grown so comfortable with living a lie and believing the lies we've been telling ourselves for so long. But traveling through the darkest parts of ourselves and facing those truths are the only way to heal ourselves properly.

People choose to run because facing the truth and change requires hard work, but when you run, you'll run for the rest of your life.

> I wasn't always happy with who I saw in the mirror. At a point in my life, I couldn't look at myself.

Take A Deeper Look.

Now, what does any of this have to do with self-love, you may ask? It has everything to do with self-love. Understanding yourself plays a significant part in the journey. How can you heal if you don't know what to heal?
The journey is much deeper than toxic lovers and relationships. The most important part of the journey is building a better and healthier relationship with yourself. You have to find unconditional love for yourself first. I came across a quote that said, "The healing hurts much more than the wounds," and it does hurt; it hurts very much. Mental, emotional, and spiritual wounds take more work and much longer to heal than physical ones. The journey back to self starts with looking within yourself and not being afraid to explore yourself. Take a deeper look at yourself. Are you proud of or happy with what you see?

It was time for me to
change my perspective
and how I viewed life and
felt about myself.

Unlearning & Learning.

The only thing that hurts more than not being happy with what you see is seeing nothing when you look at yourself. So during that period of loneliness and isolation, I worked on my mindset daily. I read books during the day and listened to audiobooks at night. I found a few YouTubers, authors, and inspirational speakers I liked and studied them daily. As they say mindset is everything. So I needed to change my thoughts and feelings about myself. Outwitting The Devil by Napoleon Hill made me realize how much of my own worst enemy I was. Reposition Yourself by T.D. Jakes taught me that there is always time to rebuild yourself. Abraham Hicks taught me how important it is to release, be in the flow, and find peace within yourself. During that healing period, I soaked up as much knowledge as possible, then applied what I learned to my life.

The more I learned, the more I started to embrace my journey. Then, finally, everything began to make sense to me. At first, I thought my life was falling apart, yet everything was falling together wonderfully.

Finding Balance.

When I finally came out of that difficult time in life, I had a better understanding of life and who I was. Without adversity, mistakes, pain, and suffering, I wouldn't be who I am. I couldn't escape darkness. I was tired of fighting it. Instead of taking the time to understand it, I gave up and let it consume me. I feared it and gave it power over my life, thoughts, and how I felt about myself and my decisions. We can't run from darkness; it will always be a part of us. Many speak of darkness as bad, but in it, I discovered myself and healed. I didn't become it, but I did learn to embrace it. I made peace with my inner demons, and we became best friends. Only after getting through it did I understand why I had to go through everything I went through. It was never meant to scare me or hurt me. I so badly wanted to heal, grow, and find inner peace. The only way to do that was to spend some time in the darkest parts of myself. I needed to find the balance between darkness and light.

Nothing happens
by mistake; we
make mistakes
God doesn't.

Right Where You're Supposed To Be.

I was no longer ashamed of who I was. There was
no more fighting with myself. My past no longer
had power over me. My inner demons stopped
tormenting me. I grew to accept myself; all of me, and
for the first time in my life, I gained complete control
of myself. The only thing better than looking good is
feeling good. I worked so hard on myself mentally,
spiritually, and emotionally. I had never felt so alive,
and this feeling was unfamiliar to me. There is a
light at the end of the tunnel, but you have to keep
going. Take the road less traveled; there's so much
beauty in the unknown. Do not fear uncertainty. Do
not question where you are in your journey because
you're exactly where you should be.

I accepted where I was
and understood why
I needed to take this
journey because the
problem was me, and I
had much more work to
do. In addition, I realized
the relationship I shared
with myself also played
a significant part in my
relationships with others.

The Problem Could Be You.

Many think they can run from the pain by jumping from relationship to relationship. Desperately looking and searching for that special someone to make them happy and feel loved and appreciated. Jumping in and out of connections from one person to the next solves nothing. It will not change the experiences; you will only keep attracting the same energy and repeating the same toxic cycle. We get so caught up in wanting to be loved and chasing love that we rarely take the time to work on ourselves or build a better relationship with ourselves. If you take the time to look deep within, you'll see where the real problems lie.

Looking within highlighted my toxic behavior towards others and made me realize how unhealthy I was to myself.

Accountability.

They say people will change when they
want to, not when you want them to. So,
I spent most of my journey self-reflecting.
I think about some of the women I hurt
and the time I've wasted. I also think
about some women I've let hurt and
manipulate me. There are no excuses for
who or how I used to be, and I have no
shame or regrets. We can point fingers
and blame everyone for how we live and
love, but there's no healing without some
accountability. So many of us do things
without thinking. After you've lived a
certain way for so long or gotten used
to specific outcomes, it just becomes
routine. We don't notice it. We become
so stuck in our ways, the toxic cycles,
being hurt, or hurting people that we get
comfortable with it.

We must own up to
our poor decisions,
behavior, and mistakes
and learn from them.

Understanding Ourselves.

When you look back at the people you've dated or used to entertain, you start to feel disgusted at yourself; like, what was I thinking? How did I allow myself to get involved with these people? Why did I settle and let people treat me wrong for so long? You start seeing things differently in the middle of your journey. Not just in your relationship life but life in general. We may never understand why things happen the way they do or why people do the things they do, but we are solely responsible for understanding ourselves and our behavior. We spend so much time trying to understand and make sense of everything and everyone but ourselves. That realization made me focus less on my relationships with others and more on my relationship with myself.

How can you live a beautiful life if you feel you're not worthy of the beautiful things life has to offer? How can you truly know what you want from a person if you don't know what you want for yourself?

You Are What You Attract.

There was no more searching for someone to love, appreciate, and complete me since I found everything I was expecting from others within myself. I began to vibrate at a much higher frequency. People and relationships I would settle for before didn't work for me. Setting healthy boundaries for myself allowed the right people to gravitate toward me. Lustful and temporary relationships weren't enough for me. I learned how to separate my needs from my wants and how to make the right decisions. I started to make more rational decisions rather than emotional ones. I understood that who you want isn't always who you need, and who you need isn't always who you like. How can you know what you want from a person if you don't know what you want for yourself? That is why the journey back to yourself is so important. To get a clearer vision of what you deserve, reflect on the relationships you used to settle for in the past and why you settled for them.

Everything in life is replaceable except for life itself. The love I have for myself has grown tremendously. Now I understand that no matter my current circumstances or failed relationships I've experienced, none of that doesn't define who you are, who you can become, or your worth. Once you realize how exceptional you are, you understand the importance of protecting and caring for yourself.

Realizing Your Worth.

When you no longer believe the lies you've been telling yourself, you realize that how people treated you in the past never defined who you are or your worth. You start to see that you are worth much more than what you've settled for, and you are worthy of healthy, unconditional love. So many of us forget we don't have to settle for anyone who doesn't have the best intentions for us. We give people and material things power over us. The journey back to self is about taking back that power, stepping into our strength, and understanding that we will always be more than enough. No matter who comes or goes or how many people have mistreated you. No matter what people say or what they see in you. None of that determines your worth.

You must learn to get comfortable with saying no without feeling guilty. It's not only part of self-care but is also self-empowering.

It's Okay To Put Yourself First.

We spend so much time wanting to be loved and accepted by others and never enough time loving and accepting ourselves. We get so used to giving and putting others ahead of ourselves that we feel guilty whenever we decide to put ourselves first. Putting myself last to make other people happy was something I once struggled with. I loved bombing people, thinking it would make them love me more. Constantly being there and doing things for people hoping it would make them appreciate me more. The worst thing you could do is search for validation from others. It's like we seek praise for being a good person and having a big heart, but what's the point of being a good person if you can't be a good person toward yourself? And what's the point in having a big heart if you're not doing what you need to do to protect it? I had to learn that it isn't a crime to put yourself first and find the courage to stop saying yes when I meant no.

For the first time, I felt I was entirely in control. The conversation you have with yourself plays a significant part in your growth. I replaced my negative thoughts with positive affirmations. Affirmations I said every morning before I started my day. It wasn't long before I began to feel good about myself.

Mastering Self.

After so many years of living with a victim mentality, I realized how much power I had over my life. I was becoming the master of my life. I found my power—you'll never give it back once you find it. I started to feel good about myself. I loved this new confidence I saw in myself. I was incredibly proud of the results I saw. The improvement and growth made me delve deeper into myself. Sometimes your most complex decisions bring forth your most significant transformations.

I dived and began
to free fall, falling
deeper and deeper
within myself.

Dive In Deeper.

A deep dive into my inner world helped me
see that it was never me against the world.
It had always been me against me. I was
losing the battle, and the only way to win
it was to dive deep within since knowing
what you're dealing with will teach you
how to deal with it.

The path you are on at the
moment doesn't matter;
life will always lead you
back to yourself.

Everything Comes Full Circle.

With a deeper understanding of yourself, you can better cope with people and problems, as well as handle adversity. You know not to panic under pressure or question why certain things are happening in your life. As I've always said, we make mistakes, but God doesn't. It took me a while to accept and understand that statement. Nothing happens by mistake.

You have to be
committed to your
journey and serious
about your growth.

Be Serious
About Your Growth.

Examine your life and the things you want to change about yourself, be it your love life or your personal life. What's keeping you from becoming a better you? Find who or what is blocking your happiness or disrupting your peace, and remove it. Whatever you struggle with in your life, focus on that. Do you think I'd be who I am without doing the inner work? I wanted better for myself and clearly envisioned who I wanted to be. So, I put all of my focus on becoming just that.

Progress is progress; celebrate your growth, no matter how big or small.

Give Yourself Some Credit.

After so many years of battling myself and doing the inner work, I'm exactly where I need to be. I'm thrilled with the person I've grown to be. Things could be better because some parts of myself still need work. We never fully heal. There'll always be things about ourselves that we need to work on. Once you've learned to accept that, accept that you'll never be perfect. You know to be a little kinder to yourself. We get upset and stressed about not being there yet, but we must give ourselves some credit for the work, time, and effort we put into ourselves. You're different from the person you were last year. That alone is something you should celebrate and be proud of. Any growth is a significant achievement. Look at your healing journey less than how long or hard it will be. You'll never begin it thinking that way. It's a process, and there's no need to rush; healing takes time. Don't focus on what still needs to be done because, in due time, you'll get there. You may not be the person you want to be now, but you're not who you used to be. You may still be hurting doing the process, but you're no longer a prisoner to your pain because you've finally found the courage to take the steps towards a happier, healthier, and better you.

The journey is much more endurable when you learn to trust yourself and understand that you'll not always have everything under control. It's better to let things flow.

Going Against The Flow.

Balance and inner peace are what I desperately needed at the time because my life was so chaotic. I didn't accept where I was because I believed I would be further ahead. We spend most of our lives trying to force things instead of just being in the now and allowing life to take its course. We try so hard to control every outcome. We fight so hard trying to avoid endings without knowing that we are only delaying that fresh beginning or shift in our lives we desperately hope for. Life is much better when you allow things to flow in and out of your life, but you must learn to trust yourself and your journey thoroughly to get into that state. It is best to accept where you are now but understand it's not where you'll be forever.

I felt like a leaf blowing in the wind flowing through life, trusting fully in my journey, not caring where I land.

Entering The Flow State.

You either sink or swim, they say. Well, I learned how to float and breathe underwater. The weight of the world was no longer on my shoulders. I entered a state of flow. I worked on everything I needed to work on and released everything I needed to remove. Before starting your journey, you need to have the main goals you want to achieve; my main goals were balance, inner peace, learning not to worry or overreact, and trusting that whatever's happening in my life isn't to punish me, but to make me a better person.

I no longer saw life
as an endless struggle;
I rather saw it as a beautiful
journey worth embracing.

Life Is Like An Amusement Park.

I stopped seeing adversity and every setback and battle as me getting punished. Instead, I started to look at them as teachers and lessons I needed to learn to become my true self. I stopped being so hard on myself for every mistake because our mistakes are only growth opportunities. Instead, I embraced life as if it was an adventure; allowing my inner child to heal made me feel like a kid again. I now see life as a theme park waiting for me to explore it, instead of an endless struggle. The journey back to yourself doesn't have to be a hard one. Instead, you should feel excited about the journey. I was like a kid running around his favorite amusement park, embracing everything life threw at me.

You can sit around and wait for someone to save you or you can save yourself.

Become Your Own Hero.

We spend most of our lives sitting around, waiting for someone to save us. We get mad at our parents for what they didn't teach us or the life they didn't give us, but at some point in our lives, when we've reached a certain age, we have to take responsibility for our own lives and save ourselves. I realized that no one was coming to save me and no one would do the work for me, so I became my hero. I got to the point where I could no longer ignore the silent cries of my soul. If you don't take the time to hear those silent cries, they will only get louder and louder throughout life. Only you can stop your suffering. I remember how long I've been trapped in prison, ignorant of the fact that I had the key this whole time; the key to happiness, peace, and freedom.

I found the key and freed myself; it was inside me the whole time.

Freedom.

You must find your definition of freedom; what does freedom mean to you? First, freedom to me is having the liberty to love, heal, grow, and be myself. Second, freedom is knowing I control my life and happiness. Third, freedom is knowing that my life only reflects and becomes my decision. Finally, freedom is living, walking, and speaking my truth. That is what freedom means to me.

There's great power inside of you, but you'll have to dive deep within yourself to find it.

Stepping Into My Power.

Life no longer had its foot on my neck, and my inner demons no longer had power over me because I demanded respect. I no longer allowed my negative mindset to ruin me. My childhood wounds were healing beautifully. I didn't recognize this new person I saw in the mirror, but I wasn't ashamed of him; I was proud of him.

I spent most of my life living in fear, but the fear I once felt was no longer there. Instead, I started to experience life like I never did before.

Ready For Life.

No more living life with my head down, no more doubting myself, no more fear, no more holding back or being afraid to shine my light. I was back, not to who I was but to a much better version of me; I started to fight back.

> For the first time, I felt I was ready for life and only hoped that life was ready for me.

The Journey.

I found a new love for life and a new love for myself; this is what taking the journey back to yourself is all about. No matter how hard the journey may seem, keep fighting, keep pushing, and keep going!

Daily Affirmations

1. I am learning
2. I am healing
3. I am growing
4. I am balanced
5. I am flowing
6. I trust the process
7. I am exactly where I need to be
8. I am releasing everything that's blocking my blessings and hindering my growth
9. I am stepping into my power
10. I am taking my life back
11. I am no longer living in the past
12. I am free
13. I am the master of my life
14. I am at peace with myself
15. I am ready to receive all that I deserve
16. I am freeing up space for new beginnings
17. I am blessed, and I am abundant
18. I am thankful
19. I am grateful
20. I am the happiest I've ever been

I am poetry, the beauty and the ugly, the weak and the strong, light and darkness, pain and love. I am all of the above — K.Rashad

When you know everything happens in God's timing and not yours, how you react is different, your trust is different, and your patience is different. You handle life, adversity, and your problems differently. You can see his hands strategically rearranging the pieces in your life. There's no need to worry when you already trust the outcome.

THE JOURNEY BACK TO SELF. TAKE A DEEP DIVE WITHIN

CPSIA information can be obtained
at www.ICGtesting.com
Printed in the USA
BVHW051101200423
662717BV00002B/117